# 2 Chronicles
# 7:14

# *Revival*

## STAN HUBERFELD

2 Chronicles 7:14 — Revival

Stan Huberfeld

Printed in the United States of America

H.G. Publishing

Langhorne, Pennsylvania 19047

The views expressed in works published by H.G. Publishing are those of the author. The author is solely responsible for the contents.

Library of Congress Control Number: 2001012345
ISBN 978-0-9801037-3-1

# Table of Contents

# Forward

A heart of thanksgiving is always a reasonable place to start. Thank you, Heavenly Father, Jesus and Holy Spirit for loving me from Day 1. Through that love, You have provided for me personally, one day at a time, one moment at a time, and will continue to do so through all eternity.

Life has provided me (and each of us) a format for learning. I have learned through the processing of information, as well as through making decisions. Some decisions have been good ones, and some have been poor. Each of us has accumulated head (intellectual) knowledge and the capability of heart knowledge. Someone once told me the longest trip I will ever take is the 18" from my brain to my heart. Pure heart knowledge is a form of love that gives 100% of itself all the time. It is Jesus Christ Himself. As I continue to apply the Word of God to my life, I realize how blessed I am through His love for me. I made the decision to follow Jesus for myself about 25 years ago, and I need to apply it in meaningful ways through each step of life. By His grace and love, I encourage you to do the same.

# Introduction

I love my country. We should all be thankful for the blessing of our nation. This is a great place to live and raise our families.

I have walked down many paths in my life. I have always been well-provided for with regard to food, housing, education, opportunities, employment and more. I have also walked down some paths of foolishness. I ignored God for years, used drugs, abused alcohol, gambled too much, disrespected women and used "my fun" as the key to decision-making. However, by God's grace, my eyes were opened to the truth and my life has changed.

I believe with all my heart that as sure as I am that Jesus is Lord, I am sure our nation needs an awakening to God. Some issues I raise in the following pages will slap you in the face – Praise the Lord! I need it, and so do you. I pray that God will reveal this truth to you and that you will be obedient to Him in a much more significant way than you ever have been in the past.

Dear Lord, in the Name of Jesus, bless our nation and begin the process of change with me. Amen.

# Some
# <u>Basic Thoughts</u>

## 2 Chronicles 7:14

*If my people, who are called by my name, will humble themselves and pray and seek my face and turn from their wicked ways, then I will hear from heaven and will forgive their sin and will heal their land.*

# The Vision

Will you take a few moments in a comfortable place and just relax?  Please consider all the segments of life that make up our society today.  How are things?  What direction are we heading?  For the most part, is it better or worse than it was 10 years ago?

I want the best for my country, my family and myself.  Simply stated, I believe we as a nation are a mess.  I do not see the best happening for us all.  The answer is not going to be found with our new President or in the Democratic Party.  Nor is the Republican Party the answer.  We are not going to find what we need in tax reform, social security, 401-K plans, or any new (or old) set of government programs.  Sad to say, the answer will not be found in our Christian churches, either.  The Christian churches in our nation are not consistently Kingdom-focused.  Each and every Christian church does some things well, some things fairly well, and some things poorly.  Because they are not Kingdom-focused, but are self-focused, their agendas far too often are inappropriate.  Things like filling the pews, meeting budget projections, being quick to point out the flaws of the church down the street, self-adulation, cover-up and denial are too often of primary interest.  Shame on us!

The answer is revival.  Discernment tells me that we have a short amount of time to be open to the change revival can bring. I have NO knowledge of when Jesus is coming back. Using all that God has blessed me with to venture a GUESS, I would say that sooner seems more likely than later. I really do NOT know. However, I can hear the clock ticking and ticking loudly.

I need revival in my own life in a big way. My need to change is not 5-10%; it is much larger than that. Every individual I know personally is in the same boat. Revival is not a minor tweaking in my life; it involves extending my arms open fully, kicking the door to my heart open 100%, full confession of my sins, and asking my God to change everything in my heart and life that is not fully of Him! The transformation will not be completed in a one-shot prayer communion because of my need for daily renewal. So daily it is, and daily it will be. As you read through this book, you too must come to grips with the same questions. By His grace, He is always there to confirm and help me.

He is patient, faithful and good. PRAISE GOD!

# God Loves You

Did you ever wonder why God, who is all knowing, all-powerful and perfect in love, bothered to make man? Maybe He needed me to help Him out? Perhaps He was a few dollars short and my contributions would balance the budget? Thoughts like these are ludicrous and clearly NOT true. Simply stated, we were made in His image *(Genesis 1:26)* for fellowship. We were the crowning achievement of creation. For five days, God created the earth, and it was described as good. On day six, man was made, and God said it was "very good" *(Genesis 1:31)*.

My mind is blown away by the fact that God loves me. If I were the only person in the history of mankind to embrace this truth, He would have done nothing differently. The depth of His love for me will take an eternity to completely understand. However, in my present status I can understand this much: Sin (which each of us has committed) was separating me from God. I was helpless to do anything about it. So God provided His plan of love. He sent His son Jesus to leave heaven, live His life as a role model (without sin), and die to pay the price (blood sacrifice) for my sins *(Romans 3:22-23 and 5:6-8)*.

I don't know about you. However, that is clearly off the chart of my ability to love. Perhaps, on my best day ever, I could sacrifice myself for you. I have two children that I love dearly; my daughter, Sara, and my son, Jesse. There is no way I could allow them to be brutally beaten, suffer unspeakable humiliation, and die to pay for your sins. Yet, that is exactly what my heavenly Father did for me and for you. Accepting the free gift of the Father's love in the person and Lordship of Jesus Christ is the cornerstone of understanding and internalizing His love.

Here are just a few thoughts that God has for you:

• Your love, O Lord, reaches to the heavens, your faithfulness reaches to the sky. – *Psalms 36:5*

• I have loved you with an everlasting love; I have drawn you with everlasting kindness. – *Jeremiah 31:3*

• For God so loved the world that He gave His one and only son, that whoever believes in Him shall not perish but have eternal life. – *John 3:16*

The gift of love is sitting there, fully gift-wrapped with a bow on top. What are you going to do with this undeserved gift you have received?

# You May Not Like Me

There are people who already know me and do not like me. After reading this book, you may want to join their ranks. That is your free-will choice.

However, you need to understand that popularity and being politically correct are not standards by which I choose to live my life. Because of who God is to me, I am attempting to deliver a message in this book. I know that my message may well be flawed. However, that is because I am flawed, which does not change one basic truth: We each must have a heart for revival.

Having a heart for revival includes a willingness to implement personal change in your life in ways that are meaningful. I have not arrived in my Christianity and neither have you. Do not look to the person on your left or on your right. Do not wait for someone else to agree with you. This is not about your church's position on the subject. There is no elder board in charge here. No committee will be formed to approve a 10-point outline of steps needed to be taken.

It is about your renewed commitment to the Lordship of Jesus Christ, over and above the walls of foolishness you have built for yourself. Thy kingdom come, Thy will be done – and start with me.

# Revival

The dictionary gives us a good overview of this word. Revival means to have been brought back to a healthy, vigorous or flourishing condition, after a decline. A stirring up of religious faith among those who have been indifferent is another way to see it.

When I hear the word "revival," my thoughts touch the base of society itself. I love my country very much. My desire is for revival to take place all across our nation. However, revival is a one-person-at-a-time issue. I must deal with myself and with God on this issue, as you must do the same. Most of us, me included, do not see ourselves as being in a personal state of spiritual decline. This is a core issue for Gentiles (non-Christians who call themselves Christians). It is also a major issue for Christians. For the record, I will explore this subject of who is a Christian in the next chapter.

So, how did this state of decline become reality? I have bought into a lie, a BIG lie, that life is "all about me." This lie is authored by our spiritual adversary himself. That's right; it comes straight from the pit of Hell. Having bought this lie, I then have allowed myself, one decision at a time, to water-down the basis of my decision making. I do this by leaning heavily on my own intellectual understanding of how things should be

*(Proverbs 3:5-6)*. This is precisely what I am warned NOT to do!

The truth of God shall set you free and here it is: I was created for the purpose of having intimate fellowship with a righteous and holy God. Because He is God, I *must* recognize and acknowledge Him also as Lord. That means He should be sitting on the throne of all parts of my life. The only way I know how to do this is to fully live a life according to his Word (the Bible), and be led by His Spirit, in combination. I *must* do both. I need to be keenly aware of my capacity to deceive myself. As the Word says, "The heart is deceitful above all things and beyond cure. Who can understand it?" *(Jeremiah 17:9)*.

I am quick to deceive myself. The state of my 401-K, the number and size of the toys I own, or whatever feeds my flesh will easily ensnare my thoughts into false thinking. This is not a condition in which my life can flourish. Life is for many thousands of years. For the sake of discussion, let's say 100,000 years. Why would any sane person base life decisions on 1/10 of one percent of that life, unless he or she was deceived? A true condition for flourishing is when I am implementing the Word of God daily. This condition is the standard by which life is and will be measured eternally. The things and stuff of me are falsehood. What good is it to climb the ladder of this earthly life and get to or near the top, only to realize the ladder is leaning against the wrong building?

There are some basic questions I must ask myself: Do I want revival in my own life or not? Am I willing to expose myself, step out of my comfort zone, and venture into new territory – to enter into places, conversations and real-life experiences where I have previously not gone, or gone only rarely? A life where every day, I am on a mission trip that includes ministry to my wife, children, extended family, co-workers in the marketplace; with neighbors, on the soccer field, at karate and youth group activities, with strangers and more? If so, my daily planner must start with prayer, end with prayer and thread prayer throughout the day. This communion with my Lord is the source of my marching orders.

Does any of this sound scary? You'd better believe it. It also sounds extremely exciting, because my God is an awesome God. He loves me with an everlasting love. Nothing can separate me from the love of God that is in Christ Jesus *(Romans 8:38-39)*. My God is Lord of all. He is the Lord God Almighty. He is omnipotent. Greater is He that is in me than any situation I will face in life.

My frame of reference for revival is my vertical accountability to Jesus. It would be great if I could have an influence on the person to my right or the person to my left. However, that issue is between them and God. I cannot allow my call to be influenced by what my church says. Organized religion has been bound up in its own sin issues for years. I am not endorsing abandoning our churches. I am suggesting that I need to be living my life according to the Word of God and led by the Holy Spirit. In this way, I can be a blessing to others in my church or any church, regardless of who they are.

I am so excited about revival, I can hardly contain myself. The best part is to watch and see what God is going to do next.

There is zero pressure on me. It is not about me. It is about *we*. I just need to draw near, be obedient and live out His direction. He does the rest. I have no bottom line of expectation except obedience. Thank you Father, Jesus, and Holy Spirit. I love you. Amen

# Who Is a Christian?

Perhaps 75% (*http://www.adherents.com/rel_USA.html#religions*) of the people in the United States of America, when asked, will say they are Christians. God has called each one of us to use our spiritual discernment. He wired us that way when He made us. We have an innate ability to be spiritually discerning. We also have free choice. So, we are fully capable of becoming callous to that discernment with our self-focused indifference.

Based on my understanding of the scriptures (and yes, I know my understanding is flawed), in combination with my discernment, I believe the large majority of that 75% of the population are NOT Christians. You are gentiles. A more symbolic definition is that you are fence-sitters. Loosely speaking, you maintain some form of mild contact with Christianity while you are actively captaining your own ship in life. If you are the captain, then who is God, second in command? Or, perhaps He works in the galley? Just saying it points out the ludicrous posture of this type of thinking. Yet, this is exactly how the majority of the citizens of our nation is living out their faith.

I had a sincere conversation with a friend of long-standing some years ago. She explained to me that she was a Christian, too. However, she has chosen not to be so "fanatical" about her faith as I. In the end, God knows she loves Him and the difference between my life and hers will be like dust. She believes that dust will be blown away by God in the final analysis. Another frequently heard assertion is that "I am a good person. God knows that, and in the end, I'll be OK." Rather than have me pontificate on this type of thinking, here are a few comments from God on:

- Fence-sitting – "I know your deeds, that you are neither cold nor hot. I wish you were either one or the other. So because you are lukewarm, neither hot nor cold, I am about to spit you out of my mouth."

*— Revelation 3:15-16*

- Wealth/Toys – "Do not be overawed when a man grows rich, when the splendor of his house increases. For he will take nothing with him when he dies, his splendor will not ascend with him. Though while he lived he counted himself as blessed and men praise you when you prosper, he will join the generation of his fathers who will never see the light of life. A man who has riches without understanding is like the beasts that perish."

*— Psalms 49: 16-20*

- Good Works – "All of us have become like one who is unclean. All of our righteous acts are like filthy rags. We all shrivel up like a leaf, and like the wind, our sins sweep us away."

*— Isaiah 64:6*

- Good Person – "There is no difference, for all have sinned and fall short of the glory of God."

*— Romans 3:22B-23*

Calling all fence-sitters!  Look, if I were God, I probably would grade on a curve, take your benevolence into account, and turn the other cheek to some of your short-comings.  After all, you are just like me.  The problem is that I am *not* God.  This standard, and any one like it, is not God's standard.  God's standard is perfection.  Then how are we to measure up?  The answer is, by ourselves we can't.  But because He loves us, He has provided a way.  "The word is near you; it is in your mouth and in your heart, that is, the word of faith that we are proclaiming.  That if you confess with your mouth, 'Jesus is Lord,' and believe in your heart that God raised him form the dead, you will be saved." *(Romans 10:8-10).*

This scripture is meant to be lived out, moment by moment.  Yes, there is a point in time when your put your stake in the soil for Jesus.  That day must be real, not just a prayer you say so you can get back to whatever you were doing previously.  For further enlightenment on this point, try *Matthew 13:1-23*:

That same day Jesus went out of the house and sat by the lake.  Such large crowds gathered around him that he got into a boat and sat in it, while all the people stood on the shore.  Then he told them many things in parables, saying: "A farmer went out to sow his seed.  As he was scattering the seed, some fell along the path, and the birds came and ate it up.  Some fell on rocky places, where it did not have much soil.  It sprang up quickly, because the soil was shallow.  But when the sun came up, the plants were scorched, and they withered because they had no root.  Other seed fell among thorns, which grew up and choked the plants.  Still other seed fell on good soil, where it produced a crop — a hundred, sixty or thirty times what was sown.   He who has ears, let him hear."

The disciples came to him and asked, "Why do you speak to the people in parables?"   He replied, "The knowledge of the secrets of the kingdom of heaven has been given to you, but not to them. Whoever has will be given more, and he will have an abundance. Whoever does not have, even what he has will be taken from him.     This is why I speak to them in parables: "Though seeing, they do not see;

though hearing, they do not hear or understand.

In them is fulfilled the prophecy of Isaiah:

" 'You will be ever hearing but never understanding;

you will be ever seeing but never perceiving.

For this people's heart has become calloused;

they hardly hear with their ears,

and they have closed their eyes.

Otherwise they might see with their eyes,

hear with their ears,

understand with their hearts

and turn, and I would heal them.'

But blessed are your eyes because they see, and your ears because they hear. For I tell you the truth, many prophets and righteous men longed to see what you see but did not see it, and to hear what you hear but did not hear it. "Listen then to what the parable of the sower means: When anyone hears the message about the kingdom and does not understand it, the evil one comes and snatches away what was sown in his heart. This is the seed sown along the path.   The one who received the seed that fell on rocky places is the man who hears the word and at once receives it with joy. But since he has no root, he lasts only a short time. When trouble or persecution comes because of the word, he quickly falls away. The one who received the seed that fell among the thorns is the man who hears the word, but the worries of this life and the deceitfulness of wealth choke it, making it unfruitful. But the one who received the seed that fell on good soil is the man who hears the word and understands it. He produces a crop, yielding a hundred, sixty or thirty times what was sown."

We are called to be His ambassadors, living out his message and bearing eternal fruit. My family has a pear tree in the back yard. How do I know this? It is because, if you stand under it in season, you will see pears. You will not see apples or oranges. In some seasons, this tree has produced more pears than in others. However, it is a tree that will yield pears. When I am truly committed to the Lordship of Jesus Christ, eternal fruit will be yielded, by His grace, through my (your) life.

Here is your choice, and it is a simple one:

A. "Praise to the Lord, to God our Savior, who daily bears our burdens. Our God is a God who saves; from the Sovereign Lord comes escape from death."                                   — *Psalms 68: 19-20*

Jesus answered, "I tell you the truth, no one can enter the kingdom of heaven unless he is born of water and the Spirit. Flesh gives birth to flesh, but the Spirit gives birth to spirit. You should not be surprised at my saying, you must be born again.

*— John 3:5-7*

## OR

B.      "May they be blotted out of the book of life and not be listed with the righteous."                              — *Psalm 69:28*

"The ax is already at the root of the trees, and every tree that does not produce good fruit will be cut down and thrown into the fire."                                          — *Luke 3:9*

### Each of us gets one choice.

Now that you have chosen, you are faced with another question.   Are you going to embrace the "my people" of 2 Chronicles 7:14 for yourself?

# We Are at War

Wake up, America! In case you've forgotten, or never realized it, we are at war. Sending troops to a given country, or recalling them, will never define our situation. America was founded as a Judeo-Christian nation. That is who we are and I am proud of it. Being accepting of others who reject our faith is OK, only in the sense of respecting their right to choose. We are utter fools if we allow this acceptance to spill over into the roots of who we are. We need to fight for our value/faith-based way of life. If not, we will lose it for sure.

Our spiritual lives and our physical lives are linked. For the past few decades, we have allowed our society to be degraded by very well educated (and probably well-meaning) people who have placed God in a second or lower position on the priority scale of life. I am sorry, but this is an abomination and needs to be exposed as such. Those of us who believe in Judeo-Christian faith values need to draw the line. Not only must we not back up one more inch, we must counterattack and retake our nation. Those of you who have been sitting on the fence of faith must choose: Is it going to be God's way or the new-age rhetoric? There is NO middle ground. If you believe there is, you are fooling yourself.

Gee, Stan, isn't that awfully narrow-minded thinking? The

answer is, no it is not. Praise God that He has given us a light unto our path at all. Since when do I (or you) deserve that? His way is in my best interest. It is paved with love and long-term provisions in full.

The new-age plan has many roads and the number continues to increase, as every one does what is right in his own eyes. However, these roads all have one thing in common: They lead to destruction and the dismantling of the nation I love! This will result in the deterioration of the quality of life I want for myself and my family. Then there is the final loss that is the eternal separation from God in a place of darkness, where there is continuous suffering, weeping and the gnashing of teeth.

One day, I was watching a show about World War II on the History Channel. A famous heathen, Josef Stalin, was wise enough to say this at Stalingrad: "We will not retreat. We will draw the line and fight the Nazis right here. Win or lose, we will not retreat." If he, who was notoriously evil and un-godly, was wise enough to see the reality of his situation, are we, the family of God, to be less discerning?

Each of us needs to receive from God targets, personal marching orders in this fight. Yes, that means humbling my heart, praying, seeking Him personally, and abandoning my own agenda while embracing His. He will be the one to coordinate our collective availability for an effective counter-attack!

Praise the Lord, if we are faithful, He will not let us fail.

# My Commitment to Action

# Our
# Old Friend (NOT)
# Sin

# Sin Defined

According to *Harper's Bible Dictionary*, sin is that which is in opposition to God's benevolent purposes for His creation. Sin is an ever present reality that enslaves the human race and has corrupted God's created order.

I will discuss the subject of sin from a slightly different perspective. The large majority of our sin problems (wicked ways) fall into three categories:

- OOZE (It's my nature)
- Leaning on my own understanding (Yeah, I get to be God)
- Trade-in

While we are discussing this subject, decide for yourself whether this scripture applies to our nation today:

"Has a nation ever changed its gods? (Yet they are not gods at all.) But my people have exchanged their Glory for worthless idols. Be appalled at this, O heavens, and shudder with great horror," declares the LORD. "My people have committed two sins: They have forsaken me, the spring of living water, and have dug their own cisterns, broken cisterns that cannot hold water." *(Jeremiah 2:11-13)*

# 3 Types of Sin

I feel confident in saying that almost everyone realizes that they have shortcomings. We all make mistakes daily — with our words, by our actions, and in our thoughts. This is no great revelation. "We must pay more attention, therefore, to what we have heard, so we do not drift away." *(Hebrews 2:11)* Since the fall of Adam and Eve, we have been under the yoke of a sin nature. This is the source of the ooze. We long to put ourselves first and God second (or no place at all). In addition, we have become very good at this while deceiving ourselves to the contrary. The truth is we just naturally ooze sin.

However, this is no justification for our current state of being. I can do something about this. Some years ago, I went scuba diving in Cozumel, Mexico. We were drift diving. The boat dropped the divers off into the water, and due to the strong current, went about a mile down-current to wait for us at the end of the dive. It felt good to leisurely enjoy the dive and progress with the current. Spiritually speaking, our nation and the world have been drifting away from God and from having a Kingdom focus. Just as there was that day in Cozumel, there is a choice to be made. If I kicked hard I could fight against the current and proceed in any direction I chose. We can do the same thing.

Even better, we have God walking with us and helping us each and every step of the way. With His loving assistance, I can change direction.

"This is the message we have heard from him and declare to you: God is light; in him there is no darkness at all. If we claim to have fellowship with him yet walk in the darkness, we lie and do not live by the truth. But if we walk in the light, as he is in the light, we have fellowship with one another, and the blood of Jesus, his Son, purifies us from all sin.

If we claim to be without sin, we deceive ourselves and the truth is not in us. If we confess our sins, he is faithful and just and will forgive us our sins and purify us from all unrighteousness. If we claim we have not sinned, we make him out to be a liar and his word has no place in our lives."

*—1 John 1:5-10*

By His love and grace, my ooze problem can be overcome. Praise God!

## Sin – Leaning on My Own Understanding

"Trust in the Lord with all of your heart and lean not on your own understanding; in all your ways acknowledge him and he will make your paths straight."  — *Proverbs 3:5-6*

I do not think that a theological dissertation is required to understand this proverb. However, what do we tend to do with the scripture? We memorize it, blend it with our doctrinal posture and then proceed to live life as we see fit. This is exactly what we are warned not to do.

"They remembered that God was their Rock, that God Most High was their Redeemer. But then they would flatter him with their mouths, lying to him with their tongues; their hearts were not loyal to him, they were not faithful to his covenant. "  — *Psalms 78:35-37*

You see, when I lean on my own understanding, I get to be God. I can do this naturally and in fact, that is exactly what I do. Not only that, it's enjoyable. I like it. Oh, by the way, it's sin in its purest form!

This problem is so rampant among believing Christians that for the most part, these sins have become socially acceptable. I am going to step out on a limb now and speak for God. I believe He is sick to His stomach over these issues. That's right, we have managed to make God nauseous.

There are a number of ways in which this sinful thinking manifests itself in our lives. Let's take a look at a few of these issues:

- Time
- Finances
- Keeping our word
- Parochial thinking
- Spiritual arrogance

This list could easily be expanded, I know. However, these certainly are some of the major issues. All of these (including themes not mentioned) are related, almost like first cousins and second cousins.

**Leaning on Our Own Understanding/Time**

We live in an over-booked, fast-paced, high-tech society. Much of that is simply fine and brings blessings to our lives and the lives of others. But stop right now. Take a look at an average day in your life from the past week. Did it include a significant amount of quality time for just you and your Lord to commune? "But those who seek the Lord lack no good thing" *(Psalms 34:10)*. I know the early hours of the morning are tough. However, you are fresh, not as easily distracted by the things of life, and it is QUIET. Early in the morning will I rise up and seek thee *(Isaiah 26:9)*.

I have often thought that time with God is a lot like eating. If you do not do it, you will be very unhealthy. Fast food (5-10 minutes with God) or the snack plan is OK. However, this is true only if it is balanced with high-quality, sit-down, family-style meals. Spiritually, these are your one-hour-plus blocks of time, including prayer, quiet time, Bible study, church and church activities. And of course, there is always the banquet or smorgasbord, which corresponds to the necessary personal retreat (not the men's or women's retreats!) that features you and God, one-on-one for 24-72 hours.

It's great if you can make the time for a personal retreat on a quarterly basis, but you should never allow more than a year to pass without this refreshment. Right now, stop what you are doing and block off some time with Him for you to be blessed. There is nothing that pleases God more than when I commit my time to just hanging out with Him. I am His child. I know how I feel when my kids want to be with me. He loves me (and you) so much!

### Leaning on Your Own Understanding/Money

Spiritually speaking, the way we handle money is not a problem before God. It is the symptom of a problem. That problem is our submission to Lordship. If you are fond of the Old Testament guideline, then 10 percent of your gross income is the minimum you should give to the Kingdom. Anything less than that is stealing from God.

"I the Lord do not change. So you, oh descendants of Jacob, are not destroyed. Ever since the time of your forefathers you have turned away from my decrees and have not kept them. Return to me and I will return to you," says the Lord Almighty.
"But you ask, 'How are we to return?'
"Will a man rob God? Yet you rob me.
"But you ask, 'How do we rob you?'
"In tithes and offerings. You are under a curse – the whole nation of you – because you are robbing me. Bring the whole tithe into the storehouse, that there may be food in my house. Test me in this," says the Lord Almighty, "and see if I will not throw open the floodgates of heaven and pour out so much blessing that you will not have room enough for it. I will prevent pests from devouring your crops, and the vines in your fields will not cast their fruit," says the Lord Almighty.
"You have said harsh things against me," says the Lord.
"Yet you ask, 'What have we said against you?'
"You have said, 'It is futile to serve God. What did we gain by carrying out his requirements and going about like mourners before the Lord Almighty? But now we call the arrogant blessed.

Certainly the evil-doers prosper, and even those who challenge God escape.'"

Then those who feared the Lord talked with each other, and the Lord listened and heard. A scroll of remembrance was written in his presence concerning those who feared the Lord and honored his name.

"They will be mine," says the Lord Almighty, "in the day when I make up my treasured possession. I will spare them, just as in compassion a man spares his son who serves him. And you will again see the distinction between the righteous and the wicked, between those who serve God and those who do not."

*—Malachi 3:6-18*


Some people believe they are no longer under the law of the Old Testament, and personally, I would agree. At a minimum, it remains an excellent guideline. However, the New Testament guideline does not teach that I can do what I want to do with the money I have, and then fund the Kingdom with a piece of whatever is left. This concept is readily practiced by many, and places you on the throne of your finances. A more accurate New Testament concept is that it *all* belongs to God. After all, what do you have that is not a gift from Him? I believe that an in-depth review of your finances is a great way to apply the Word of God to your life. Seek the Lord (including godly counsel), on a line by line basis with regard to your income, budget and spending habits. He has promised to meet your needs and is faithful to do so. We become uncomfortable when we relinquish our wants and use that money to fund the Kingdom.

This is part of the humbling process. God knows our hearts' fondness for money. Some years back, I had the opportunity to share on the subject of money at a local church. In my preparation time, the Lord gave me an idea that I implemented. Each person at the gathering received a jumbo zipper locking bag in their kit/folder. Before we started the teaching portion, I asked each person to place in the bag (which now had their name on it) all of their cash, credit cards and jewelry. The bag was then sealed tightly. Now came the fun part.

Each person brought his bag to the altar and placed it in a large box. As the teaching ensued, I asked people how they felt now. Here is a sampling of the answers I received:

1. Very concerned about the bag. "Will I get the bag back?"

2. Many expressed a feeling of freedom. "I think I can hear this teaching better now."

3. People were open and more focused.

At the end of the teaching portion, God had me select two people at random to alphabetize the bags and return them to the rightful owners. Even this part of the process had some classic God elements. One of the two people I chose was, unbeknownst to me, a first-time visitor to the church. Also, following the teaching, we had a time of one-on-one conversation. Afterward, I was made aware that three people forgot to get their bags and had to be sought out individually so their belongings could be returned.

If you allow yourself to be still and meditate on this issue, you can then freely walk in obedience.

## Leaning on Your Own Understanding/Keeping Our Word

"Let your yes be yes and your no be no." *(Matthew 5:37)*

I love the simple things of life. The Bible is just that – simple enough for me today and deep enough for me to grow in for the remainder of my life. Failure to honor this principle of keeping our word, saying what we mean and meaning what we say is at an epidemic state in our culture of spin doctoring today. We qualify and justify everything to fit our own agendas and desires. We are supported in this sin by a society that says it's OK to please ourselves first and foremost. Personal **honor** and **accountability** are values that are dwindling in importance and in visibility. Instead, we are told that a watered down version of truth and integrity is just fine. Erosion of this principle in our lives and in society is a pillar that supports the reign of our spiritual adversary, whose name is not worthy to be mentioned.

Here is an idea (although not a new idea): In your daily walk, speak less – a lot less. Use the pauses to pray on the spot and seek the Lord. Then, when you do open your mouth, your words will be more godly. Once you speak, be prepared to fully **honor** what you say. The days of saying what sounds "Christian" or what is popular should be gone. Seek the Lord, speak in truth and love. Let your yes be yes and your no be no.

## Leaning on Your Own Understanding/Parochial Thinking

Parochial means "restricted to a small area or scope; narrow; limited; provincial."

There is a lie, right from the pit of Hell itself that must be exposed. It is this: "My church is better than your church." I love my church. However, the truth is that my church is not better than your church. Neither is your church better than mine. This lie, which has been around for years, is intended to increase our congregation's attendance (in numbers) and decrease yours. This is hardly a Christ-like concept. It has been justified by each church coming up with its own set of measurement standards and then using them to verify the outcome they want. This is typical of man's sinful nature and should be confessed as such. Ask yourself these questions from a more kingdom-focused perspective. Give me the name of the church that went to the cross and died for my sins (and yours). Give me the name of the church that has, at any time, lived out the Word of God perfectly. Which church allows the Holy Spirit to reign freely, in conjunction with the Word of God (the 66 books of the Bible)? Give me the name of the church that sits at the right hand of God the Father.

Our churches are flawed and always have been. Yes, I understand that people, by their nature, are sinners. However, I also understand the principle of spiritual growth. That principle allows for the total commitment to the Trinity, including the Living Word (the Bible). Stating that one has made this commitment is fraudulent unless a real, alive framework of **accountability** is in place. Instead, our churches have substituted other systems:

1. Effective cover-up of the truth (i.e. child molestation or theft of funds).

2. Elders (clones) who mimic what the pastor wants to hear. (Their job is to provide accountability for the church body and free the pastor to teach and lead the body.)

3. Benevolent pastoral dictators, where dissent is met with dismissal. (No accountability to anyone.)

4. The Word of God has been changed to accommodate whatever someone wants it to say (i.e. acceptance of homosexuality).

5. Church law, customs and traditions are placed on a par with, or in some cases, above the Bible's teachings (i.e. communion is only for members of *this* church, or adding scriptures other than the 66 books of the Bible, and treating them as the inerrant word we have received from the Lord. *(Revelation 22:18-19)*.

Any one of these scenarios is grossly unacceptable. Much of our population in the United States has seen this hypocrisy and uses it to justify their own posture of staying away from God, thus allowing themselves to be lords of their own lives. When asked, the overwhelming majority of these people call themselves Christians. Unfortunately for them, they are not. They will never see heaven or receive God's blessings unless they open their hearts to the truth of the love of God.

I would be remiss if I did not emphasize a very important fact. Even though our churches are flawed, we are commanded in the Bible to operate within that framework (our churches) for an improved Kingdom-centered result in our personal lives and in the collective body of Christ, the church. Yes, I must attend and support growth in a solid, Bible-believing fellowship. Wherever I am in my spiritual journey, and wherever my church stands spiritually, we must both embrace the truth of God's word and be desirous of change; change that will be more Kingdom-focused, not just more sets of rules or traditions. Each of us has the same calling. There are no "Lone Rangers" in the body of Christ.

Where do I go from here? Scripture tells us that "If we claim to be without sin, we deceive ourselves and the truth is not in us *(1 John 1:8)*." But, if we confess our sins "he is faithful and just and will forgive us our sins and purify us from all unrighteousness *(1 John 1:9)*." If we seek the Lord, He will make straight our paths. Be open to accountability, confession, asking forgiveness of all concerned, course correction in our lives, and a thankful heart. I must humble myself, pray, seek Him and be prepared for redirection from my own wicked ways. Through all of my foolishness, God still patiently loves me.

**Leaning on Your Own Understanding/Spiritual Arrogance**

Arrogant is defined as "full of or due to unwarranted pride and self-importance; haughty or conceited."

I define spiritual arrogance as that fine blend of spiritual head knowledge and my fleshly reign. It is somewhat like brackish water — one half is salt water, one half is fresh water. It cannot help itself; it is just that way – brackish. The truth is I need to be better at understanding the Word of God. I have not mastered that subject. Improvement in *applying* the Word of God has even more room for improvement. I have not yet arrived spiritually. You, my brother or sister, unfortunately, are just like me.

But, unlike brackish water, I can help myself. When I allow, by God's grace, my head knowledge to become heart knowledge, this sin is substantially mitigated. Due to my nature, I will never have pure heart knowledge this side of heaven. I can seek to continuously increase the percentage of heart knowledge and decrease the percentage of head knowledge. The key to this is His lordship in meaningful ways. "He must increase and I must decrease. *(John 3:30)*
Avoidance of this issue will not assist in "Thy Kingdom come." If we keep doing what we have been doing, we will keep getting what we have been getting. My heart aches for my country to be blessed. I know that the answer is Jesus and His lordship. Step one starts with me, allowing Him to reign more freely in every nook and cranny of my life, with no preconditions. When I am faithful about this, will He not hear from heaven and forgive my sin?

Thank you, Father, Jesus and Holy Spirit for being just who You are.  Help me, please, and bless our nation.

### Trade-In

I consciously make the decision, or by my nature allow the decision to be made, to trade in lords one for another. That's right, I trade in the Trinity: The Father – Jehovah-Jireh (Provider, see *Genesis 22:14*); Jehovah-Nissi (Banner, see *Exodus 17:15*); Jehovah-Shalom (Peace, see *Judges 6:24*); Jehovah-Rapha (Healer, see *Deuteronomy 32:39*); Jehovah-Shamma (Presence, see *Ezekiel 48:35*); Jehovah-Tsidkenu (Righteousness, see *Jeremiah 23:6*) – the Son (*Yeshua ben Josef* – Jesus) – the Holy Spirit (*Rosh Hakodesh*). All three, in their majesty, beauty and love, are traded in for that moment to serve another god. This is the god of ME, which manifests itself in many forms such as lust, anger, gluttony, etc., — to reign over me for that moment. This lord does not love me; it only wants me in bondage. This lord does not have my best interests in mind; it only wants to subjugate me. This lord does not want me to receive an eternal reward; its desire is to crush my spirit. Each time I allow this lord to reign, I make it easier for another such incident to take place.

This lord has no power at all on its own and is really NO lord at all. Its only reign exists because I set it on the throne of my life. What a fool I am! "The heart is deceitful above all things and beyond cure. Who can understand it?" *(Jeremiah 17:9)*

**How do I fix it?**

When (not *if*) I allow this sin to happen, I must be quick to recognize my poor decision and repent. That's right, it is my decision; I did it and I must take ownership of it. I can fix it, but only with the help of Jesus *(Yeshua)*, the real God, who loves me *(John 3:16* and *1 John 1:9)*. Repentance is a combination of confession and a change of direction. I need to confess on the spot or at the closest moment available, then apologize to any offended party. If the offended party grants forgiveness, praise the Lord! If the forgiveness is offered with qualifications (or not at all, which is the same thing), praise the Lord. "Brothers, I do not consider myself yet to have taken hold of it. But one thing I do: Forgetting what is behind and straining toward what is ahead. I press on toward the goal to win the prize for which God has called me heavenward in Christ Jesus." *(Philippians 3:13-14)*

Then I proceed with living my life, with God on the throne, placing those things in the rear view mirror of my mind and forgetting them. This mirror is very valuable with regard to safety when I am driving my car. But in the realm of spiritual reality, it is not only totally worthless, it drags me down. I must forget the past, understand that I have truly been forgiven by God, and walk the walk, one step at a time. God can, and will, take care of the rest. If it seems like other people are living their lives holding onto other thoughts, their circumstances should have zero impact on me. It may hurt to see it. My feelings may be hurt. But I need to remember that others are sinners, too. God is still working with each one, right where they are.

Regardless of what they are or your relationship with them, it is going to be OK because Jesus really is Lord of all. You can take that to the bank; the Eternal Savings Bank.

Thank you Father, Son and Holy Spirit, that I really am forgiven. Each day (moment) really is new, as are your mercies. Thank you, Lord, that you really are there to help me each step of the way, because I can't do it by myself. You will never leave me of forsake me. You love me with a perfect love and truly are my best friend.

"My commandment is this; love each other as I have loved you. Greater love has no one than this, that he lay down his life for his friend. You are my friends, if you do what I command. I no longer call you servants, because a servant does not know his master's business. Instead I have called you my friends, for everything I learned from my Father I have made known to you." *(John 15:12-15)*

# My Commitment to Action

# Take a Break

Let's pause for 15-20 minutes. Just sit quietly at the feet of Jesus and ask Him to reveal His message to your heart regarding these thoughts so far.

Once you have done this, prayerfully ask Him how you may apply, not less than one and not more than two, things He showed you are needed. If your heart is convicted of more than two, just take the top two for now. In a few months, you can initiate number three or number four.

Thank you, Lord Jesus, that you are faithful to lovingly show me the truth and assist me in applying it into my life, one breath at a time.

# My Commitment to Action

# Hearing From God

## Hearing God/Why Bother?

If I am to take seriously my commitment to 2 Chronicles 7:14 and revival, then communication is a key element. The word "turn" indicates moving in a new direction. Hearing from God is essential in knowing which way, when, and how much to turn.

On numerous occasions during the past 25 years, I have heard brothers and sisters in Christ say: "If only I knew what God wanted me to do!" Or, "I really need to hear from God." Most times, they would say "I really haven't heard anything." So instead, they look for His input through circumstances, comments of other people, or even their feelings. There is a better way, and I will share that with you.

If you are looking for some new revelation, a doctrinal breakthrough or a theory to end all theories, forget it! The answer to "why" is found in a simple fact that you already know. God loves you. You may need to look long and hard into your inner being to find this. However, it is in there. You may, in fact, find it easier to believe than some others and yet are saying to yourself, "I still do not hear from God," or, "I only hear from God through the pastor's sermon." Perhaps you only hear from God when you are reading his Word, the Bible. There is more, a whole lot more! The Holy Spirit is not on vacation, nor so busy that your answer is on back-order.

God doesn't just love you within the framework of your understanding of the word "love." The fact of His love for you is an open tap, holding back nothing. "While we were still sinners, Christ died for us" *(Romans 5:8)*. "This is love, not that we loved God, but that he loved us and sent his Son as an atoning sacrifice for our sins" *(1 John 4:10)*.  He loves you from your head to your toes.  His love for you is much more than an intellectual understanding.  His love permeates every cell in your body.  The hub of this relationship is in your heart.  The Holy Spirit will enable your heart to be linked with His.  And yes, God wants to use your brain and even your dreams, too.  He is the one who wired you.  And, by the way, God frequently colors outside the lines.

Try this little exercise for a few moments.  Close your eyes and take a deep breath.  With your eyes closed, imagine you are standing by the ocean's edge.  The water is rippling in waves over your feet.  There is no one else in sight.  As you open your eyes and gaze out over the expanse in front of you, you breathe deeply.  A wave of quiet encompasses your entire being.  In that quiet, you hear a still, small voice say, "Everything you see, from left to right and as far as the horizon, represents only the outer edge of my love for you."  As you allow that truth to wash over you, you come to grips with the meaning of life.  The meaning of life is simply knowing who you are in relationship to the fullness of God – that fullness being God the Father, God the Son and God the Holy Spirit – reigning in your heart as both Savior and Lord.

The God who created all this desires a personal relationship with you.  Communication is one of the pillars of any meaningful relationship.  What better relationship is there than someone who loves you with a perfect love?  You come just as you are, trust Him, avail yourself to His lordship, and He does the rest.

If you have a better plan, please write to me. I would like to know what it is. If you sense a tug of war going on inside you at this moment, who is at either end of the rope? I know God is at one end. The other end could be our spiritual adversary, your pride/selfishness, or both. Let go and let God. Trust fully in His perfect love and truth; it will set you free to hear from Him.

## Hearing God/Be Prepared

God's portion of your personal relationship is not in question. It is not a variable. He will always do His part. But in order to hear God better, you must be ready to love Him back. Any relationship with one-way or lop-sided love is doomed to have problems. He asks that you love Him with all your heart, soul, mind and strength *(Matthew 22:37 and Deuteronomy 6:5)*. This is not a casual, take-a-pill deal. This involves a permanently ongoing investment of time on your part. Spend time reading your Bible. Commune with Him daily and regularly throughout the day. "O God you are my God, earnestly I seek you. My soul thirsts for you. My body longs for you in a dry and weary land where there is no water" *(Psalms 63:1)*. "Here I am. I stand at the door and knock. If anyone hears my voice and opens the door, I will come in and eat with him and he with me" *(Revelation 3:20)*.

Take the time. Make the time to process what He is saying. Ask Him to assist you in doing that processing. You cannot do it by yourself. Your nature will be prone to, once again, lean on your own understanding. Trust Him fully and grow where you are. His blessings for you are to be found in your current life's network of relationships and circumstances. Tomorrow will take care of itself. For today, draw near to Him and He will draw near to you.

"Come near to God and he will come near to you. Wash your hands, you sinners, and purify your hearts you double-minded".

— *James 4:8*

There are times when it is good to be a Martha, doing the work. It is every bit as important to be still, sit at the feet of Jesus as Mary did, learn, and then be obedient.

As Jesus and his disciples were on their way, he came to a village where a woman named Martha opened her home to him. She had a sister called Mary, who sat at the Lord's feet listening to what he said.   But Martha was distracted by all the preparations that had to be made. She came to him and asked, "Lord, don't you care that my sister has left me to do the work by myself? Tell her to help me!"

"Martha, Martha," the Lord answered, "you are worried and upset about many things, but only one thing is needed, Mary has chosen what is better, and it will not be taken away from her."

— *Luke 10:38-42*

In the morning, O Lord, you hear my voice, in the morning I lay down my requests before you and wait in expectation.

— *Psalms 5:3*

Quietly and consistently seek Him.  Be open and prepared for obedience.  He will do the rest.

## Hearing God/Implementation

Great! You have set this time aside to commune with God in a quiet place.

> The LORD said, "Go out and stand on the mountain in the presence of the LORD, for the LORD is about to pass by." Then a great and powerful wind tore the mountains apart and shattered the rocks before the LORD, but the LORD was not in the wind. After the wind there was an earthquake, but the LORD was not in the earthquake. After the earthquake came a fire, but the LORD was not in the fire. And after the fire came a gentle whisper.
>
> — *1 Kings 19:11-12*

What's next? Please remember, this is a relationship, not a formula.

Try this idea. My one-on-one time with God is like a hot date. I am sure each of you has experienced a time when you couldn't wait to be with someone. You had great anticipation about being with this person. Your emotions were abounding. There is great comfort in knowing that is precisely how God feels about you. This personal fellowship is the very reason He made men and women. Just like a hot date, nothing is going to stand in the way of this special time slot. It is also Holy time and is to be revered as such. Instead of wearing my finest garments, I will clothe myself in His righteousness. That means confessing all of my sins, one by one in detail, and asking for forgiveness in the name of Jesus. The need for a quiet place is imperative (no cell phone). The last thing you want is to be interrupted. Your available length of time should be as open as possible. One-half hour is probably a minimum. Hours are better, and days are best.

"Do not be in a hurry to leave the king's presence." *(Ecclesiastes 8:3A)*

"I love those who love me and those who seek me, find me." *(Proverbs 8:17)*

"Let us go early to the vineyards to see if the vines have budded, if their blossoms have opened and if the pomegranates are in bloom – there I will give you my love." *(Song of Songs 7:12)*

Enter into His presence believing His purposes are good and come first.

"Why spend money on what is not bread and labor on what does not satisfy? Listen, listen to me and eat want is good, and your soul will delight in the richest of fare." *(Isaiah 55:2-3)*

Remember, your purposes need to come last.

You must desire His thoughts.

"'For my thoughts are not your thoughts. Neither are your ways my ways.' declares the Lord." "As far as the heavens are higher than the earth, so are my ways higher than your ways and my thoughts than your thoughts." *(Isaiah 55:8-9)*

Your heart needs to be open and flexible. Be prepared to have Him change your heart to be more Christ-like. He needs to be Lord of all my "stuff." "For those God foreknew he also predestined to be conformed to the likeness of his Son, that he might be the firstborn among many brothers." *(Romans 8:29)*

You need to believe you are going to hear God's voice.

"The watchman opens the gate for him and the sheep listen to his voice. He calls his own sheep by name and leads them out. When he has brought out all of his own, he goes on ahead of them and his sheep follow him because they know his voice." *(John 10:3-4)* "My sheep listen to my voice, I know them and they follow me." *(John 10:27)*

Each of these verses underscores the need I have to decrease so that He may increase. I do not need more of Stan, I need more of Jesus.

Perhaps most importantly, you need to remember that there is going to be significant opposition to this initiative to hear God. The main problem is you (or me). We love to be in charge. Our pride is masterful at deception. "The heart is deceitful above all things and beyond cure. Who can understand it?" *(Jeremiah 17:9)* Frequently, my heart's desire is my plan, with godly wrapping paper all around it to make it appear acceptable.

In addition, we have a spiritual adversary who will try, in his limited ways, to lessen this effort. He will have an effect. But you and Jesus together will carry the day. Remember, it is not about "me."

You can and should be straight-up with God. When asking Him a question, ask with a heart of thanksgiving and with the expectation of getting an answer. "Let the wise listen and add to their discerning and let the discerning get guidance." *(Proverbs 1:5)*

Be prepared to be obedient. "Do whatever he tells you."

*(John 2:5b)* Your honoring of His lordship is a beautiful thing. This may include appearing foolish (to man, not to God), or doing unorthodox things. "They came to Bethsaida, and some people brought a blind man and begged Jesus to touch him. He took the blind man by the hand and led him outside the village. When he had spit on the man's eyes and put his hands on him, Jesus asked, 'Do you see anything?' He looked up and said, 'I see people; they look like trees walking around.' Once more Jesus put his hands on the man's eyes. Then his eyes were opened, his sight was restored and he saw everything clearly." *(Mark 8:22-25)*

Ask for boldness. Absolutely desire His direction. This is pivotal, because He has a big-picture, kingdom perspective that none of us has.

There are occasions when you will set the time aside, seek the Lord in a godly way, and still not hear anything. What should you do?

Wait joyfully and stay the course. You can ask God if there is a problem area, such as unforgiveness or unconfessed sin. Sometimes you just need to wait. Thank Him for the wait. When reading Daniel 10, we are told that Michael, the archangel, was dispatched by God as soon as Daniel prayed. However, Michael had to fight the forces of the evil one for 21 days until he could reach Daniel to minister to him. Be praiseful, maybe even sing Him a song or two or three …. Telling Him of your love is always a good thing to do.

I am reminded of a story of a friend of mine who was faced with a serious question regarding his life's direction. He sought the Lord in prayer for many months and heard nothing. His spouse and others close to him did the same, and still there was no clear answer. After about a dozen challenges from me to go to the park alone, he did just that. It was a cold day, and he proceeded to walk, and walk, and walk. He prayed; he confessed; he tried to be still, and still he just continued to walk. After about 1-1/2 hours, he had heard nothing from God, and he dejectedly walked back to his car. He opened the door, got into the car, took off his hat and gloves, and exhaled a deep sigh. In that moment of exhaustion, with all of his emotions depleted, the Lord spoke to him and gave him his answer. Praise God, He is always faithful!

Heavenly Father, Jesus and Holy Spirit, I love you. Help me to be obedient in my relationship with You and in the application of your word in my relationships with others. Thank you.

### Hearing God/Verification

So, I believe I just heard from God. That is both exciting and scary. How do I know I really heard from God on any given issue?

There are a number of guidelines for this confirmation:

• We have the Bible, which is the inerrant Word of God. What I just heard will never be contrary to God's Word. "In the beginning was the Word, and the Word was with God, and the Word was God." *(John 1:1)* "We are from God and whoever knows God listens to us; but whoever is not from God does not listen to us. This is how we recognize the Spirit of truth and the spirit of falsehood." *(1 John 4:6)*

• God has, by His grace, hard-wired our being to hear from the Holy Spirit. *(John 10:3-4)* This is His desire, *(Revelation 3:20)* and He is omnipotent.

• This is the job of the Holy Spirit, who gives us peace (yes) or lack of peace (no). Galatians 5:22 tells us peace is a gift that can only come from God.

• God has given us a spouse, the *echaud* (oneness) of marriage. Share and pray with your spouse. Listen to her (him). Your partner is a special blessing in this oneness from God Himself.

• A carefully and prayerfully selected prayer partner or personal council of advisors is another avenue for verification. Please remember, receiving feedback of three (yes) to one (no) is not a green light to proceed, unless you must make a decision at this moment, due to a time constraint. The Holy Spirit will work in the hearts and minds of all who are committed to the faith.

• A carefully and prayerfully selected pastor or member(s) of a Bible study can also provide needed accountability and verification.

• Evaluating events after the fact will allow you to see clearly God's goodness and purpose. "And we know that in all things God works for the good of those who love him, who have been called according to his purpose." *(Romans 8:28)*

• After you have diligently sought the Lord, there comes a time when you just need to step out and put your feet into the water. This is called faith.

When the children of Israel reached the Promised Land after 40 years of wandering, they found the River Jordan at flood stage. It wasn't until they put their feet into the water that God miraculously stopped the water and allowed them to enter into their promised blessing.

"So when the people broke camp to cross the Jordan, the priests carrying the Ark of the Covenant went ahead of them. Now the Jordan is at flood stage all during harvest. Yet as soon as the priests who carried the ark reached the Jordan and their feet touched the water's edge, the water from upstream stopped flowing. It piled up in a heap a great distance away, at a town called Adam in the vicinity of Zarethan, while the water flowing down to the Sea of the Arabah (the Salt Sea) was completely cut off. So the people crossed over opposite Jericho. The priests who carried the ark of the covenant of the LORD stood firm on dry ground in the middle of the Jordan, while all Israel passed by until the whole nation had completed the crossing on dry ground.          — *Joshua 3:14-17*

The revival process is a daily, ongoing process for each of us. Humbling, praying, seeking and turning are all actions we need to take in order to fully embrace the notion of being God's people. Praise the Lord I have the Word of God as my guide. The natural outcome of this personal relationship is a better-directed and focused Stan. Hearing God clearly is an integral part of this improved kingdom focus.

# My Commitment to Action

# Let's Get a Second Opinion

This text is of the original prayer delivered January 23, 1996 by Pastor Joe Wright to the Kansas House of Representatives in Topeka.

Heavenly Father, we come before you today to ask your forgiveness and seek your direction and guidance.

We know your Word says, "Woe to those who call evil good," but that's exactly what we've done.

We have lost our spiritual equilibrium and inverted our values.

We confess that we have ridiculed the absolute truth of your Word and called it moral pluralism.

We have worshiped other gods and called it multiculturalism.

We have endorsed perversion and called it an alternative lifestyle.

We have exploited the poor and called it the lottery.

We have neglected the needy and called it self-preservation.

We have rewarded laziness and called it welfare.

We have killed our unborn and called it choice.

We have shot abortionists and called it justifiable.

We have neglected to discipline our children and called it building esteem.

We have abused power and called it political savvy.

We have coveted our neighbors' possessions and called it ambition.

We have polluted the air with profanity and pornography and called it freedom of expression.

We have ridiculed the time-honored values of our forefathers and called it enlightenment. Search us O God and know our hearts today; try us and see if there be some wicked way in us; cleanse us from every sin and set us free. Guide and bless these men and women who have been sent here by the people of Kansas, and who have been ordained by you, to govern this great state. Grant them your wisdom to rule and may their decisions direct us to the center of your will. I ask it in the name of your son, the living savior, Jesus Christ.   Amen.

# Take a Break II

Please consider this a MUST assignment: Before you proceed with me one more page in this book, go to your favorite quiet place (i.e. the park) and spend one hour with God. Take NOTHING with you — especially NOT your cell phone, Bluetooth®, IPod® or headset. That's right, one hour of just you and God. If for any reason you fall asleep during that hour, you have failed the assignment. In that case, repeat the process.

You will be blessed. "Come near to God and he will come near to you. Wash your hands, you sinners, and purify your hearts, you double-minded." *(James 4:8)*

"Therefore brothers, since we have confidence to enter the most holy place by the blood of Jesus, by a new an living way opened for us through the curtain, that is, his body, and since we have a great priest over the house of God, let us draw near to God with a sincere heart in full assurance of faith, having our hearts sprinkled to cleanse us from a guilty conscience and having our bodies washed with pure water. Let us hold unswervingly to the hope we profess, for he who promised is faithful." *(Hebrews 10:19-23)*

The purpose of the exercise is to meaningfully set revival into motion in my own life. I have no idea what He wants to tell *you* personally. However, I am 100% sure that if you will humble yourself, pray and seek His face, He will bless you with a message of love that is personal and meaningful to you.

Before reading any further, go and be blessed.

# My Commitment to Action

# What Do We (I) Do from Here?

### Humble Myself

Humble is defined by Webster as: Having or showing a consciousness of one's defects or shortcomings; not proud, not self-assertive, modest; to reduce the arrogance and self-dependence of; to be meek and submissive to the divine will.

T.S. Eliot said "Humility is the most difficult of all virtues. To achieve it, nothing dies harder than the desire to think well of oneself."

The first thing to be considered here is which side of the fence of life you are on. Is it God's side or your side? There will not be one fence-sitter in the Kingdom of Heaven. Choose this day whom you will serve.

"But if serving the LORD seems undesirable to you, then choose for yourselves this day whom you will serve, whether the gods your forefathers served beyond the River, or the gods of the Amorites, in whose land you are living. But as for me and my household, we will serve the LORD." *(Joshua 24:15)*

I don't know about you, but I find "humbling" unattractive and difficult. That is because my initial reaction is focused through the eyes of self. Yet, Jesus promised He would never leave me or forsake me *(Deuteronomy 31:6 and Hebrews 13:5)*. So, I need to call out to the Lord, in the name of Jesus, and say "I can't do this 'humble' thing by myself. Would you please help me?" I truly want revival in my own life and for my country. It is the only option available to us for the future. The present course of our lives, our churches and our nation just will not cut it. A new president, new legislation, a new pastor, new elders, or new programs are NOT the answer. Hearts changed by the Holy Spirit is the answer. He will honor His part of the relationship; of that there is no doubt. I am the variable.

I must understand this about myself: I am a man influenced by emotions, and frequently those emotions betray me. I am also the one who falters in my implementation. We all do. That is why it is a good thing to remember accountability after my initial commitment to revival. Yes, first and foremost I need to implement whatever changes He shows me about my own life. I cannot and am not called to change anyone else. Some of the best guidelines for personal accountability include:

- Daily prayer.
- Daily time in the Word of God.
- Daily quiet time. (This is perhaps the least used by Christians, and yet is exactly what Jesus told Martha about Mary – just sit at His feet and be still!)
- Spouse time (prayer and sharing).
- A regular prayer partner.
- Be active in a small group (Home Fellowship/Life Group).

Each of these guidelines is a godly principle that develops depth of relationship in both a heavenly and an earthly realm. Through all of this, allow God to be your Lord. "Humble yourselves before the Lord and He will lift you up." *(James 4:10)*

Maybe we would all be better off if we just adopted the heart of a teenaged Jewish girl who said, "I am the Lord's servant, may it be done to me as you have said." *(Luke 1:38)*

# K.I.S.S.

Let's just "keep it simple and sane."

If you will just pause for a moment and reflect on who you are and who God is, one obvious reality comes to mind: We make things way too complicated. We deal with too many issues, and usually try to tackle them all at the same time. First, we have our great volume of acquired knowledge. Then we blend in our projections, emotions and desire to be accepted by others. It is no wonder we make ourselves *meshuganah* (Yiddish for *crazy*)!

Then there is God. He is as deep as all of the universe. Yet, He keeps things beautifully simple. The Pharisees were trying to trip Jesus up when they asked Him, "'Teacher, which is the greatest commandment in the law? Jesus replied, 'Love the Lord your God with all your heart and with all your soul and with all your mind. This is the first and greatest commandment. And the second is like it. Love your neighbor as yourself.'" *(Matthew 22:36-39)* This is simple and easy to understand. What about the rest of the Bible and religious doctrine? He answered that in the next verse, Matthew 22:40: "ALL the law and the Prophets hang on these two commandments." I love it. He takes hundreds of pages of scripture and puts it all into a few sentences that anyone can understand.

Furthermore, God, in His greatness, has wired each one of us with the innate ability to be plugged in to the spiritual reality of life. Each of us has been given the choice for good (God's way) or evil (any other way). This will be the roadmap for our lives.

Fatherhood has been both a huge blessing to me and a challenge. Each of you parents is well aware of the many curveballs your kids will present to you. Some years ago, God gave me an answer for the deluge of scenarios that arise in child-rearing: "It is never wrong to do the right thing."

There is much peace to be found in keeping things simple and being obedient to God. You may opt for Plan B, but there will be a reckoning for each one of us. "Do not be deceived: God cannot be mocked. A man reaps what he sows. The one who sows to please his sinful nature, from that nature will reap destruction; the one who sows to please the Spirit, from the Spirit will reap eternal life. Let us not become weary in doing good, for at the proper time, we will reap a harvest if we do not give up. Therefore, as we have opportunity, let us do good to all people, especially to those who belong to the family of believers." *(Galatians 6:7-10)*

Are there thousands of variables and challenges in my life? Yes, there are. This is where the rubber meets the road with regard to revival in my life. However, the last time I checked, my life's walk is achieved one step at a time. My prayer and focus is toward the next step. Two steps or 2,000 steps down the road will always be there, waiting. My next step is the one that can truly impact the outcome of my life. If that is not easy enough, my best friend Jesus is there to help me take that next step. That is beautiful, easy and blessed – by His grace.

# Stop at the Fueling Station

I know this walk of life is challenging. In fact, the challenges are greater than all human resources I am able to muster in response. The good news is I am not on this road or in the battle alone. Praise the Lord!

Well, where is this fuel depot? Where do I go to find it? Again, God's simplicity is so beautiful; it is right where you are at this moment. Try this, wherever you are at this time. Extend your arms outward, palms up. Close your eyes and take a deep breath and say a short prayer, maybe one like this: Dear heavenly Father, in the name of Jesus, I love you. I am unable to meet the challenges facing me by myself. Please bless me, by Your grace. Amen.

- "He gives strength to the weary and increases the power of the weak." *(Isaiah 40:29)*
- "But those who hope in the Lord will renew their strength. They will soar on wings like eagles; they will run and not grow weary, they will walk and not be faint." *(Isaiah 40:31)*

The need for refueling occurs many times each day. The first reason is that my fuel tank leaks. Secondly, He wants me to depend on Him continuously. It can be compared with the children of Israel in the desert for 40 years – their provision was daily. They were unable to horde the food from the previous day. God was faithful to them. He is faithful today. He has no intention of changing who He is tomorrow, and He will not.

I know God loves me *(John 3:16)*. I know God is faithful to who He is (Trinity and Word). I know that together, I will receive His power to address any situation that faces me in this life and throughout eternity. "No, in all these things we are more than conquerors through him who loved us. For I am convinced that neither death nor life, neither angels nor demons, neither the present nor the future, nor anything else in all creation, will be able to separate us from the love of God that is in Christ Jesus our Lord." *(Romans 8:37-39)*

Dear Father, by the power of the resurrection of my Lord, Jesus Christ, give me the strength, boldness, wisdom, discernment, sensitivity and love that I need to meet the challenges I face, for today.

# Getting from Where I Am to Where He Wants Me to Be

I am at the point in my spiritual life where some fundamental building blocks are in place.

1. I am saved by grace.

2. I understand my life is totally dependent upon God. Everything I have or am is a gift from Him.

3. The desire of my heart is to be Kingdom-focused.

4. I am committed to the fact that the Bible (all 66 books) is the inerrant Word of God.

5. I seek to be led by the Spirit in every situation, relationship and conversation of my life.

Then what is missing for my personal revival? What is missing in my life is the same thing that is missing in yours. I have been unwilling to take the steps to get from where I am now, spiritually, to where He wants me to be. My heart is deceptive *(Jeremiah 17:9)*, and I need to fight past it. My sin nature (arrogance, pride and other characteristics) is too healthy. I cheat God out of sufficient quiet time. I am too concerned about what others will say and think of me. Instead, I need to come to grips with the reality of the fact that I stand before a righteous and holy God TODAY. I will be called to account in heaven for what happens today. A heart totally surrendered to the application of His Word in my life, is where I am called to be.

That's right, revival is about implementation. Jesus said, "If you love me, you will obey my commandments." *(John 14:15 and 1 John 5:3)* Possession of head knowledge, and even heart knowledge, without works is worthless (reference the Book of James). "If my people, who are called by my name, would humble themselves and pray and seek my face and turn from their wicked ways, then I will hear from heaven and will forgive their sin and heal their land." *(2 Chronicles 7:14)* Revival of our churches and our nation requires commitment from one person at a time. It will not come from the top down. It will happen from the bottom up.

I must do my part and God will most certainly do His. In this process, I will falter. Here again, "He is faithful and just and will forgive us our sins and purify us from all unrighteousness." *(1 John 1:9)* The process of repentance, which follows confession, requires a change of direction. As I set into motion some new steps for myself, these steps must be honoring to His marching orders and will always be Kingdom-focused.

I have been receiving direction with regard to my own life.

There are two things I am able to share. First is that I have taken the time and resources required to write this book. Because I am not a full-time author, this is no small commitment. In addition, this book is likely to get some people upset with me because it is an "in your face" type of communication. But as sure as I know that the sun rises in the east and sets in the west, that is how sure I am that God has called me to this authorship.

The second thing I can share with you is you need to do the same thing with regard to making receipt of His direction priority number one. Ask the Lord what the steps are that you must follow. And then honor them. These steps may include a compilation of existing ones, ones that need to be tweaked and new ones.

I am not foolish enough to think that I (or you) will ever complete this journey while I am alive. It is a journey that repeats itself, moment by moment, step by step. However, the desire of my heart is to make my next step the right one. To seek Him (Word and Spirit) and implement that into my life that He has placed in front of me. I must do this intentionally, one day at a time, one moment at a time. When I do this, He will increase in me and I will decrease. At this time, I would like to give tribute to some of my favorite role models in scripture: Shadrach, Meshach and Abednego. These guys were not superstars. They were everyday guys, just like me and you. Yet when faced with the fire of life, they simply took a deep breath, sought the Lord and were obedient.

"Shadrach, Meshach and Abednego replied to the king, 'O Nebuchadnezzar, we do not need to defend ourselves before you in this matter. If we are thrown into the blazing furnace, the God we serve is able to save us from it, and he will rescue us from your hand, o king. But even if he does not, we want you to know, O king, that we will not serve your gods or worship the image of gold you have set up.'" *(Daniel 3:16-18)*

Dear Lord, forgive me and help me. I need to be more obedience-focused and not as outcome-oriented as I am. I know in the deepest part of my heart, it is not about me. I need to be, by your grace, much more Kingdom-focused. Simply stated, that means to be obedient to the call of your love. Thank you, Lord Jesus.

— Stan

# Share the Vision

I have sought to share my heart with you regarding revival. I fully understand that I do NOT know when. Jesus is coming back. Perhaps His return is today, and maybe 10 to 20 years from now. More than 20 years is a number about which I personally have less peace. However, I sense in my spirit that we as a nation have one last chance for revival. It is right now.

Revival will come one heart at a time. Your church may support whole heartedly, casually or not at all. Churches tend to be afraid of great workings of the Holy Spirit. After all, without church oversight, guidelines, elders or a committee, who is in control? God, Himself, is in control. Praise the Lord!

Please prayerfully consider this. Set into motion only that which the Lord shows you personally. Do not water down that which He shows you, even a little!

Please make sharing this vision a priority. This can be achieved in many ways:

Be open, be bold, and be obedient.

Thank you, Jesus.

# Additional Information

This book was written because of my love for my country and my Savior. It is my passionate belief that our nation and our churches must wake up and re-ignite the fire of Pentecost, leaving our complacency behind and truly taking hold of what it means to be God's people and representatives in our society today.

Your feedback and inputs are greatly encouraged. You are welcome to contact me at stanhuberfeld@gmail.com, or through H.G. Publishing.

You can also follow and comment on my blog about revival, which I believe is fundamental and vital to every Christian in these times. Join me on the blog!

E-Mail: stanhuberfeld@gmail.com

Blog: http://2chronicles7-14pray.blogspot.com/

H.G. Publishing
301 Ellis Road
Langhorne, PA 19047-1376

## More from this author!

*Walking With God* chronicles some of the events in the life of an ordinary Jewish businessman that led him to an understanding of God's deep and constant love. It is the story of how acceptance of that love changed a life devoid of meaning to a life overflowing with joy, purpose and peace. Each chapter vignette offers insight into God's love and caring, as the author takes his first tenuous steps toward turning his life over to God's will rather than insisting on his own. On the way, he experiences miraculous healings, prophecy, and a host of new beginnings that bring more meaning and richness to his life than he ever dreamed possible!

Meet Stan Huberfeld, born in Philadelphia, PA to Jewish immigrants who raised him in the traditions of that faith. He is not a scholar but a businessman, husband and father whose life experiences, personal Bible study and spiritual journey led him to a profound belief in and reliance upon God through Jesus Christ as Lord, Savior and best friend. His relationship with Christ is personal and abiding, guiding his everyday business and personal life.

## What the readers are saying...

"I can see how this book can not only call a non-believer to a place of faith and belief, I also believe it can be a great encouragement to Christians who could use a reminder of the powerful ways that God works in our lives." -- *Chris, Newtown, PA*

"Reading this book opens my eyes to what it means that our God is the same today, yesterday and forever." -- *Victor, Cameroon, Africa*

"It was a challenge to me to be more open to what God might be wanting me to do at any time. Thanks for being obedient." -- *Dave, Boston, MA*

"Know that your book, which I read during my hospital stay, was a great source of comfort, rest and encouragement." -- *Bob, Athens, GA*

"Thank you so much for sharing your blessing and being a blessing to me."
-- *Dave, Northfield, NJ*